I hope you are

happy ...

— AL Franie

I hope you are

happy ...

HeartBreak PSA

— AL Frankie

Introduction:
Last night I dreamt that my heart was not big enough
For all the people in it.
I cried until dawn.

Elaboration:
Last night I dreamt that my heart was not big enough
for all the people in it.
I woke up
Weeping.
I remember so vividly,
My fingers tearing into my open chest,
Trying to stretch out my heart,
Squeezing and pulling at the ventricles,
So I can fit my loved ones in.
But the more I stretched
The more I found myself fearful
To think that I would be forced to pick between you.
How can I endure this agony?
I do not love you all the same
I love you differently
This barbaric fate has given me such cosmic
radiance in forms of individuals
And nothing but a fist-sized human heart
Just to be torn
So you can live in it.

I cried until dawn.

Courage PSA

At some point, you will say to yourself:
"It's time for them to discover my art."
Your focus will become unclouded,
your existence no longer timid.

You have so much soul to share
but you have been a hoarding hourglass
grasping it
like sand against your chest.

Let it spill through your pores
and slip through your fingers.

If your pride bursts like a fruit
when they stomp the grapes of your labor,
let their feet pulverize the flesh of your imagination
into the sweat,
for your passion has been an everlasting fever
into the blood,
for there is an itch on the inside of your bones to
create and you have been scraping yourself raw
into the tears,
for all the plentiful criticisms they will have for your
talent
as if they plowed the sweet soil of your mind and
reaped your harvest.
Just remember,
that is how you make wine.

Stillness PSA

I have been taking photos of us
by taking photos of strangers.
This whole time
I have been looking for you
in the most foreign of places.
I wanted to
lock the moments inside a lens,
where we are still alive.
The two of us
inside the frames
Unchanging.
One day I will look at this 4x6 inch
and it will be the only place
where I found myself
Happy.

Truth

How often
In the midst of loving you do I think to myself:
"This too shall hurt"

Cautious

You can tell we are both children of trauma
In how carefully we make plans
We are used to futures that are inconsistent
Instead of the ones that we deserve
You are scared to whisper
I want you here
What if I overhear
What if you plea to make me stay
And yet I still leave

"I was her."

Will you love me?
I am so unsure of myself.

I have fingerprints like cracks
in the paint of old piano keys.

Every time I touch you,
My fingertips ring
Like there is static inside of me

My mind is an off-tone music box.
If wound, it is capable of raspy melody
To you, it sounds unfamiliar

My eyes smell like wet pavement,
They have seen many feet
walking away
In their puddle reflections, they let a little light in.

My heart is a snap of guillotine,
Will the sharpness of my decisions
Cut into the fabric of how I am making you feel

The rough skin on knees, from when I was a kid.
Scabs and bruises so frequent,
they had no time to heal.

I grew into a woman
shaped like a coke bottle,
I used to kick with my feet.
Careful, I am 5 feet and 9 inches of glass.

I don't have much to my name but
memories of a girl who played in the dirt,
coming home with the hands of a coal miner.

Will you love her?

Blind

While looking for love:
Put your trust in someone.
Close your eyes.
Feel for the world with fingertips.
Feel the weakness in your knees.

Every move will feel closer to an abyss.
Hope,
That you will hold hands with someone
who will clench their fingers
against your forearms and pull you up
if we were to stumble.

Yet,
You might encounter pitfalls
while intertwining fingers,
Your partner is also in the dark.
And since both parties are without sight,
One often does not know if the other
Is palm to palm with someone else.
Blindsided,
You might run your toes into sharp edges of betrayal.

Do not cling to
someone who sinks into the solid ground.
For it is hard to walk alongside
Someone whose embrace
Weighs heavy like a leaded jacket.

Next Steps

I am so scared that this will ruin us
If I am not happy
I have a gift for sabotage
of ruining most precious stuff
exchanging all my blessing for some shitty luck
just so I have my freedom back
even at the cost of misery.

Every rope has an end

You said:
"after each time I thought,
I still want to be with that person"
But what if
One day
We reach the point
When we are both
way too exhausted
to keep on trying
to move the skyscrapers we have
growing in-between our clasping hands.
And freedom seems so liberating
and peaceful
who knew that solitude can be so lethal
when it pushes up against
our love and pinches it into submission

Without each other
We could once again breathe easy
All the memories of us
Could give way to new beginnings
With some new
Unhurt
And unfamiliar with the bullshit
But will you fight for us
For all we were once
For all we could be again
For all the passion in our memory
Or will you walk
Because sometimes just saying
"it's not meant to be"
is easy

Dear Lover:

Bear with me.
I know too well, the act of being left
I know too little, of the act of being loved.
I may ask too many questions
I may try to fix the problems that may not yet exist
I may start to put your happiness above mine.
Don't let me.
Nature made me a romantic
Life made me into a pessimist
If fate gave me a gift as good as you
Then surely there must be pain hidden underneath
I look for it because it's all that is familiar
The self-inflicting hurt and feeling incomplete
How could I get used to someone caring for me
When no other lover did
But I have made a vow that you are the one
That I won't give up on
That I will make it work until we are both exhausted
and used up and hating each other
And only then will I let go.
I won't let my previous misery control my outcomes
The way I sabotaged myself a thousand times before.

My Tender Touch

I wonder if my fingerprints are fine enough to sand
away the abrasions on your skin.
So you can finally look in the mirror
free of scars
and see yourself
as whole as the ocean.
I am either going to fix you for the next girl or
I am going to ruin you.

Data Driven

You think in numbers and statistics
I think in actions and smells
It scares me that you put me in boxes
Vessels aren't made to contain chaos
This is where probability fails

Maybe these are red flags that it's not meant to be
Maybe there is someone who will want 120% of me
Maybe these are white flags that no one will
Maybe I am meant to drive you crazy
Or maybe it will drive you away

My Only Ask

Men with euthanized hearts,
broken men with calloused hands and absent fathers
become inanimate fathers.
Thick-skinned and hardened
they are there in the name
on a cashed paycheck
but like the paper they are feelingless.
They will tell you to stand tall
and will teach you how to hold your tears back
but not how to hold on to love
or how to let go of loved ones.

I hope one day you hug our son
I hope he grows up without fear of affection.

The poem with three meanings

Life gave you lemons.
It gave me rotten fruit.

The forecast says
there will be rain on your parade.
The sun just won't come up for mine.

You have been dealt a crappy hand at cards
I can't play the games from which I have been
disqualified.

Life gave you lemons
It also gave me you

Warning

If this comes to an end,
Please know,
I have scratched off my nails.
Did you hear me outside your door?

Lust PSA

What is lust but a craving for affection in the most intimate of places? After all, who ever gets the access to the crevice of your mind? What is lust but a plea for understanding, disguised so masterfully behind the camouflage of flesh? The body is such a foe to the immaterial, like grains of truth dissolving in a warm lie. How can we deny the need for being more than self, connecting to another entity? The need to touch is only there to soothe the acidic fear of abandonment. How could they leave when you are reaching them? What is lust but something very primitive, born out of the atomic need to gather particles, the cluster of attraction became the congregation of the universe? Your need to move closer to your opposite is simply the making of the cosmos, your matter lusting to reunite with specs and fragments of itself. What is lust but an excuse to allow yourself to freely seek the wholesomeness as you amass the essence of another?

Awakening

I want to be more than just the fruit around the pit
Or maybe I just want to be worshiped
Maybe I just want you on your knees
Kissing on my thighs and in-betweens

Oh, so this is what it is like to break a heart.
To be on the other end of pain inflicted
You should be scared of me because I may be too
smart
But you are scared that I may be too pretty

You won't believe me if I say I never played around
But I only started writing stanzas days before I met
you
Intuitive, I know the right way to show affection
While tying knots around your ankles, so you have
nowhere to run

I'm just here to eat you up with my big bright eyes
And you'll get lost in them so easily
Thinking of how they are innocent and sweet, but
Plot twist: I am innocent and sweet

Lustful Poem

Let's give in to the violence
Of all this:
The push,
The pull,
the screech,
Lust's muted whisper.
So in the morning when I leave your magnetic bed
it is a struggle to keep living.

A little more 'touch me'

Here I am:
Butterfingered
thoughts running like
ants on melting brown
sugar. Breasts, flushing
in hot spell and
swelter under your breath.
Elbows curving around
my back as
you unzip me.

Sur-r-ender

There are worse ways to spell doom
than to have you trace your fingers like a cobra
underneath my chin and kiss me silly.
Surrender can be an act of heroism.
Mid-sentence, suspended by a breathless comma
Why hesitate or defer intimacy
Why lick the edges when you can sip sweet opium
resign yourself to the mantra
of my quiet whisper: stay

Womanhood

Hummingbird flies near
a lagoon of a lotus flower
now they become one

Infatuation

You were
A girl like the weather.
Unpredictable, despite what the experts said.
You made poor judgment and cigarettes cool.
I never thought I could enjoy being in a presence
of something so powerful yet volatile.

There may be no God.
No life after death.
No real purpose to
this meaningless universe but a random accident.
Why then would I not try to taste you?

Saccharine

A single peck is all I need. One touch and my lips are
to awaken
Snow White's sweet, strawberry plump lips
that hide behind the glass case.

Who needs the poison of nutritious apples?
Evil witches should have thought of the candied
tarts.
I want to soak my fingers into your honey.
Every lick and bite, a sugar rush.

Today it's a parfait of intimacy;
tomorrow I hope to never sober up
The morning after is only unwilling delirium.
I had so much fun, kissing with my eyes open.

Bedsheet Profound

Outside is cold
And we are here keeping each other warm.
This is also a metaphor.

Fairy Tales PSA

I don't believe in soul mates
I believe in efforts
you either put in or you don't

You say you don't know
if you are the one for me
but I like you now and perhaps
indefinitely

I don't believe in happy endings
Unless I die first
and I don't spend a day without your love

You don't need to be my everything
but I want you to be my veteran
hold me steady and endure
faithfully

Morbid Lovesong

my sweet darling,

am I dreaming?
is before me a handsome image
of your familiar face?

how could this be,
when I have surely
just this evening
taken my concluding breath?

Hush my dearest
pause your speaking
will you kiss me sweet instead?
Part your lips together slowly and press your teeth
into my neck

My sweet darling,
I have not seen the sun in days
I just can't seem to get warm under this moonlight
my body craves the sunshine rays

Hush my dearest
don't you dare draw the drapes,
there is a storm behind the window
Just lay your head upon this pillow, I will be your
sweet escape

My sweet darling
when you touch me
all I feel is a burning blaze
when you cradle me so gently, you set my skin
aflame

Hush my dearest
I am feverish
I've become so gravely ill
that is why my touch is scorching your translucent,
pale skin.

My sweet darling
where is our child?
how I yearn to hear it cry
I feel no movement in my stomach
my womb feels so dry and empty,
I'm afraid that so am I

Hush my dearest
you will never have a son
but unlike those real lovers
we shall not become undone
come here dearest, kiss me sweetly
it is time, that I confess
all we have is but each other
under tender death's caress.

Passing Notes

I can show you an endless summer.
There is an entire world left undiscovered.
Let's get drunk off those reckless kisses
We don't gotta wait now, till the class dismisses
I am a grown woman, I live wild and freely
But we can still have young love, best of both worlds,
really
Let's wait till it's dark and sneak out the window
Whisper on the phone like we got secret info
Reckless abandon is always in season.
Worshipping each other is our new religion.
Love doesn't come willingly,
You gotta go and get her.
And I got no time for a "see you later"
So here is your chance to call me baby
Please check one box

☐ Yes ☐ No ☒ Maybe

You know who you are

I woke up next to you
This morning
A warm lazy shiver crawled along my shoulder like
a drunk centipede
If this goes on
I won't have anything to write about
All of my material is heartbreak
This new feeling is foreign
It's unfamiliar
Your love will ruin me as a poet

How it becomes real

"Things are getting serious"
the spectators will note
when you start to spend time together without
needing to plan it out
or when you start to call them yours
or when you move in together
but none of that will seem compelling enough to
raise your adrenaline level
into that existential mood of yours where you start to
ponder
"Is this right for me" or "is this really what I want"
after all. All of those "serious" things just seemed like
a natural sort of progression.
One day you will drive down a winding road or it
could be a highway of sorts or a back alley
and it will be raining or it might be a cloudy or a
bleached, sunny day.
You behind the wheel, them absentmindedly staring
out the window and half-listening to the radio. At
that moment, they are wearing that disposition that
indicates how comfortable and relaxed in your
presence they feel. Like nothing could ever hurt
them.
They will jump out of their reverie, their hand will
outstretch in swift motion turning up the volume on
the radio.
"This is our song!"-they will laugh and shake their
fists excitedly. You will turn to look at them as if you
spent these years with a stranger and today you are
finally introduced.
Your insides will turn, there will be a slight but
constant shiver on the edges of your skin and the
only response you will manage to produce for them
will be "Okay."
And they will continue the exuberant celebration of
their discovery and you will be sitting there
mindlessly rolling through the earth in shock.
And that's it. That's the point of no return. It's not the
meeting of the parents or the shared bank account or

expensive trips or thoughtful Christmas presents.
You can find those things with someone else.
It's this song. No one would dare possess it again.
They already took it. They stuck a flag in it. It is them
now.
The choice for you behind these windshield wipers is
not how quickly or where you can push the breaks
but whether you decide to accept that you have
arrived.
Or move on.

The Vows

I want to see this to the end
One day we may run out of love
Your fingers calloused, tired from touching skin
so freckle filled
and thin, from time pulling it
tight
around my face.

One day my fickle heart
may jump aboard the vessel
abandoning the ship
that carried it
and along with it into the depths I go
impulsively.
If loving is just a game against time's tide
and one day it will drag you down.

But maybe we are lucky enough to
ride
like foam
against a sandy shore
and each year older
have you brush my cheek
and polish it like glass.

Friend's Wedding

When I first noticed your love
I didn't not recognize it.
I was fooled and pickpocketed and left for dead
before.
I never met your love.
I never seen, proud love.
I watched it closely as it had stones thrown at it and
it stood there unflinching and unfazed.
My skepticism was dripping sweat, like sap from a
broken tree
but it could not contaminate your love.
I threw sand in the eyes of your love,
but it still looked at me.
I beat it with bricks and nails.
I screamed:
Save yourself.
Run!
But it stood there, no bruises forming, not a single
droplet of blood. Wholesome. Proud.
Your love.
It pulled me in by the hips and held me there while I
trembled.
It asked me: why are you shaking?
I answered:
"I don't know who you are"
I was shaking away the armor,
it was cracking around me
as if it was built out of dust.

Your love has washed my feet.
It healed my scars and blisters.
We dined on wine and cheese.
It listened to my stories.
It told me: "You have traveled far. Stay awhile."
Your love looked at my hands, on all the lines and
wrinkles and it traced fingers alongside them.
I asked: "What do you see in my future."
It gave no reply but a kiss on my palm.
I went to sleep next to it, our feet melting together
like glass coils, our skin polarized against each other.

Your love played with my hair and kissed my neck and kept me warm.
I felt so inexperienced I became anxious of sleep.
What if I close my eyes;
What if when I open them I find a cold empty bed with an imprint of love,
its ghostly figure still there
but the warmth is gone.
What will I do with my arms?
What will I do with my hands?
After all. I was fooled and pickpocketed and left for dead before.
But the sleep found me and your love held me and rocked me like a hammock.
And each day I open my eyes and find your love cradling me like safe harbor hugs a ship when it arrives at the shore.
And it's here.
It's still here

Deathbed

You. Are my deathbed.
Your name has carved itself on the inside of my
veins.
You. Are internal bleeding
I bite my tongue when someone mentions love.
You. Plan a slow, deliberate killing:
A touch of your eyelashes,
Brush against my cheek,
And my spirit shivers
Inside my skin, arteries, and tissues.
Creeping in the corner of my eye
I can not unsee you
Closer and closer
in my peripheral
capturing and closing in.
I moan,
I reach the ending of my rope,
You are my deathbed.
Oh, how I wish that I could lay in silence inside your
cold embrace.

Say No To Happy Endings

I would never want to die in your arms
To have you hold my breathless body
That life stepped out of,
And have your mind imprint an image of my skin
losing warmth under your lips
as you hastily try to kiss it back to life,
and my vacant stare filled with absence
And have you cry out to me without an answer
wishing to hear me fracture silence
just once more.

On Loving

Loving without delusion
is knowing that they had a life before me
and they will have a life after me
and knowing that you can not break
or build someone with your mere existence.
I am not a period that all sentences end with
and if I or our love meets a tragic end
like all humans, you will learn to survive without
me.
But,
neither am I a comma.
for I was not made to fill up spaces
or connect the dots
or fill up time.

Your mind will circulate back to me.

For you have tasted a peach that fell
from an apple tree
a fruit like no other.

Drought PSA

Due to recent drought conditions
the facility will provide love upon request only.
Additionally, we have implemented a coordinated
response plan, to decrease the irresponsible usage of
love and potential shortages.
Our conservation measures include but are not
limited to:

- Frowning upon any displays of affection
  from surrounding parties
- Making sure that apparatus is clamped tight,
  to prevent leaks
- Avoiding romanticism or romantic themes
- Embracing the notion of being a third wheel
- Avoid encouraging flirtatious attention
  especially during the heat of the day.
- Remaining cold and unmoved until it
  evaporates.

Please use love wisely.

Young Love

I used to love him
I do admit
But that was many years ago
And I was a different person
then.

And she has not survived.

Pen Pal

If you want to write me a letter
then please write it ón my skin.
I'm still waiting on a response from you
Trace your fingers, deep

There is no return address
On the time that passed us by
I was trying hard to read you
I was left with paper cuts

I long to ask for your forgiveness
But I make no apologies for feelings
I developed without meaning
to lead you astray

Love that's loved alone

Love that's loved alone
Is loving wasted.
A single bright orchid in a shaded garden,
Waiting for a hummingbird.
It blooms at dusk and leaves a scented trail.
As autumn comes it will wither dry in hope.

Belly Flop

It always seems to sneak up on me.
At first, I only put my feet in
Then you smile at me and I jump into a puddle
You make a splash
And I skip a heartbeat.
And I get used to your water,
And all of the sudden
I am
Knee deep
Waist deep
Neck deep
And then I am covered.
When I see bubbles,
I know I am holding my breath.
I realize this wasn't testing the waters.
I can drown.

Nuances

I don't like the word maybe
I like the word perhaps

I don't like the word boyfriend
I like the word partner

I don't like the word you
I like the word us

I don't like the word sexy
I like the word sensual

You don't like the word committed
You like to keep it "casual"

Happiness is not a linear equation

As time goes by
With your hair grey
You'll think of days
when you were young.
Your heart was
never touched by pain.
You planned to spend
your future and a day,
Chasing laughter
to the edge of time,
Just so she
won't ever need to cry.
At some point
you must have learned
The human need to disappoint,
And in such a perfect creature
you have found an ordinary fault.
You discovered that you can be in love
and alone.
You snapped your fingers
and learned to dissipate.
Ripped out whatever strings she played inside your
heart.
You challenged fate!
But as years pass
You find your footprints, not your feelings,
fade.
And you think of how
The whole world is always turning on its paws
grinding its nails into dust,
But back then
she had her mouth filled up with love.
You rationed kisses
and she always asked for more

A single thought
Will still turn the corners of your mouth
Some had the wealth, the wars, the world
But you had
her

Cold Shoulder PSA

The pain of rejection
hot like a comet raging with heat

If only tears could soothe the blistered heart
that you have left out in the sun

On Being Left

You dropped me like a sugar cube into a teacup
and watched me dissolve.

Seeing you out of the corner of my eye
used to turn the corners of my mouth.

I guess on a scale of mattering
to me you were a gold bar,
to you I was a feather.

So easily you could blow me off,
as if I had no weight at all.

On Leaving

If I ever give up on loving you
You won't see a declaration of independence written
in my blood
Or hear the same screams being torn from my
windpipe
Like you did when I was still fighting for us.
No.
I will leave less of me behind.
Less hair on your clothes
Less clothes in your drawers
Less scratches on your back
Less kisses on your hands
Less words of affections
Less days spent together
Until you will find that
You have dried up an ocean of my outpouring love
for you
And your feet were never wet.
You will wake up without us.
Your memory of me will be a sand in your bed and
salt on your lips.

Allegory of our affair

Admiral of abrupt absences
abandoned me ablazed and absent-minded
in abstract absinthe aspiration,
alternative to agony.

Second Lead Syndrome

I would trade all my freedom
in a moment, for a chance to make you stay.
Lock me into your eye gaze
and throw the key away.

I'm in a shitshow with my heart
and you are in the background,
smiling,
as you're pulling all the ropes to lift the curtain up.

I may act so unaffected
but I won't receive any awards,
for this familiar role I am playing,
I am standing on this stage alone.

I was once an understudy
For a broken hearted girl
As I choke in blinding spotlight
while you clap and scream:
Encore!

On Losing Friendship

I looked into the jagged rocks cut out of time
The dusty canyon towers looking over me
Defying gravity and reason.
Dry as a husk was the air
In-between the holes carved out by storms and flash
floods
But that was thousands of years ago.
As I trace back the geographic history of our
relationship
I keep reminding myself
There used to be water here
I keep looking for it
But it just cracks in the dirt.

Harvester PSA

I will feed you
until the creek will dry up
you will sip my serum
my syrup
my spirit
until I am no longer sweet
chewing up my fibers
and shitting them out
This is why women turn bitter
and why their kisses turn tart
You have picked all the plums
from the fruit tree
and my crown has dried up.

Why have I chosen this forest to live in?
I felt freer in the hostile flats

You Make me Small

Give me
some room with Air
I ask
You give me some cold sweat
and distress
Give me
Some time to digest
I taste
Bitterness in your tone
and disgust
Give me
silence without an echo.
I'm uneasy
when all I can hear is my pride
defending itself.
Give me
some room with Air
you take all the space
with yourself

The love story of elements

In a past life you must have been water
In that fable, you have bewitched me
And I was a spark that loved to boil you up
With me, you could expand yourself
With me by your side, you became a tempest

They warned you against playing with fire
For I need air to exist
My flame can not breathe inside you.
And now I find you in human form
And you still suffocate me

Thoughts

Are my haystacks full of needles?
because I keep finding you

Thoughts#2

I am tired of chasing the same ghost
Do I have to teach you how to love?
I know my worth

Batteries not included.

I once met an engineer,
who told he was trustworthy of anyone's equipment.
I told him that I suffered from heart failure
and the machine inside my chest is much outdated.

He said that he would take a look at it
and started playing with the gears.
He needed to jump-start the engine,
to make my operating system run without
impairment.

He asked me for the key,
to wind the mechanic heart of mine.
I told him to pick it with a bobby pin,
The key is lost,
but
the components are rotating almost properly.

He questioned if I could just let him in.
I was reluctant,
fearing that the organ was beyond repair.
He would drag me to the lab
And torture me with theories.
I wished he would have listened
and noticed I was barely ticking.

He said he had no time for a Rubik's cube,
he had to figure out his own designs.
How quick he was to drop the project
when he didn't get his way.
It takes longer than a day
to make a masterpiece.

I once met an engineer
Who pledged his trust in scientific inquiry,
That left my chest with a broken instrument
But it still sings louder than your flesh heart,
without a battery.

Heartless

You play girls like instruments
you bend their bare backs
until their straws break open
spilling all their guts and feelings
on the floor
where they were covered in your semen
just two weeks ago.
Now they are covered in black tears
scratching out their calendar
between dates and pregnancy scares.
You look for freedom by delicately breaking things
and I am just another tally on the jail walls
inside your throbbing temples
next to all the others you left drained and dripping
innocence.

For yours was carved out of gravel...

I bet it's nice to have your heart be made out of stone.
Nothing can penetrate it.
A tree can not grow out of a rock.

My heart is a bottomless pond.
A tiny pebble makes a million ripples,
tall waves are crashing in a storm.

Your heart is untouched Martian sand waste.
I wonder if you are capable of love.
My heart has a million fish.
I grow attached to all of them, so quick and restless.

Like Dry Chestnuts

Like dry chestnuts,
Life keeps cracking me between its teeth.
I am a green moss that attaches itself to everything.
Open like a window on a humid summer day.
I am discarded by the host.

Taylor Swift

Men have a tendency to find traces
of themselves in my words,
pulling out double meanings,
accusing me of hidden criticisms,
when I absentmindedly make a generalization.
Finding patterns and similarities
between unrelated events,
reading between the lines
over
and over
again.
The sheer vanity to relate everything back
to themselves.
If we date, you will think every
poem I have written
was written about you
and every poem after is a cry for
attention to get your attention.
As if you were my sole muse,
the ink in my pen,
the clay molded between my fingers,
the model behind the David.
If you plan to live in fear
of me putting you on blast,
recounting our fights,
or your sexual performance
and being hunted for the rest of your life
as the Lewinsky of the creative world,
As if my art will redefine who you are
And you will live in the shadow of my publication
that means you never understood my mind and soul.
So don't look for yourself in my words
You won't grasp the real meaning.
And you should never love a poet.

The Damn Honesty

I have been staring at ceilings a lot
Because I have been bending my back for you.
I have become a slave to compromise.

I am so afraid that
you will be nothing but new material for my poetry.
And I was feeding a bottomless pit
And I wasted courage
Saying I love you.

Looking back

When you met me
Did you see my eyes like goblets
Waiting to be filled with tears
There is such a difference between wanting to love
And wanting to be loved
You were a fire
And I just wanted to sit next to you and get warm

Revelation

Turns out you only loved being loved
Like a baker that loves to bake but doesn't taste his
food
You chewed me up without swallowing
You killed me without leaving me
You left me without ever being there.

Break Up PSA

Let the weight of those words
Crush your chest into this naked mattress
Where all the sheets are crumpled up
This is where love was made
This is where love is unmade

Let yourself breathe between the sobs
Clutch your sheets and hug the pillow
Marking the lack of their embrace
You circled back to where you started
Alone

You can't wiggle yourself out of misery

Seek some comfort in the thought
And that perhaps the only thing that you can depend
on is
That tomorrow
There will be
pain
Again.

Ode to Heartbreak

And then I watch me go under
into the rabbit hole when I almost climbed my way
to the top.
One look from you and I stutter
One look from you and you squeeze my heart like a
sponge
Perhaps, love will die if I starve it,
Rationalizing, "mind over matter", teaching myself
not to hope.
I'm in a net. Now, you have caught me.
My mind has splinters from the times that you were
running my brain.
I wish I had a choice to participate in a failure.
I wish I had a chance to make a mistake, but you
kept me at length
And I wish I learned lessons other than
that I no longer trust myself with a pair of brown
eyes.

You must have thought

Kindness must come with a catch!
Caught up in keeping me from caring
Kept trying to untangle my coils and find a fault in
me

Constantly, cruising from pain to paranoia
Pulsating in fear of the past
Your personal problems peeling away at your ego

Perpetually purring for your attention
I really put all my cards in one pile and
I was ready to show you my hand.

Do not worry about the scrapes you left on me
I grew up slipping on ice
I don't need your validation
I can pick myself up.

Jilted Generation

We value distrust
Trust nobody
is our motto
When I mention vulnerability
You give me a look of disgust
Always have your guard up
Push everyone away
Because you can't push away past

Old wounds still hurt like fresh cuts
We never let go of our doubt
Suspicious of kindness and wary of warmth
We only expect a cold shoulder
instead of a shoulder to cry on
Friends can be foes
but lovers are fiends
never letting anyone near your heart
because you don't want to let them know what it
needs

Happy

Happy,
You made me feel,
like a dog hanging outside of a car window.
I wanted you to take the leash
and give this stray, a warm bed to sleep in.
Happily unaware to all the foreign warning signs
I followed you around.
But you have never learned
to keep your two hands on the wheel,
and drove us both
into a collision.

Inside of her

And I thought If I drink
enough
of this liquid, sugar stuff,
she would be sitting next to me
on this couch, where we used to fuck.

And your face and your hair won't look like a
stranger's
and if I close my eyes
I can have my three years back.
Baby, that's how they call you right?
You look so much like her...

My drunk fingers feel on your body
because I'm both thirsty and hungry
for something
This anticipation and the build-up just
before I cum
is the only moment I forget
how I miss not being fucked up.

When you open your legs
gently stroking my ego,
the warm fever rushed over my body
felt just like four weeks ago.
Oh, how I am craving that feeling.
I'm almost in love with you
but something is missing.

When I'm inside of you
something feels alien
and the way your pussy tastes is a bit different
If I shut my eyes tightly
all I see is her face
and I can only climax
If I whisper her name.

I'm way too gone
for apologies to be sounding sincere
I'm just trying to drown myself
In weed, pussy, and liquor.
I need to be doing a little more cumming
And a little less thinking
~~Of how I fucked up~~
~~Of how I can't even fuck~~
of her.

I am an old soul, with a young heart in a slowly aging body

Youth is for the wasted.
Stumbling over ourselves,
looking for salvation as if answers
can be found
if you drink enough amber
and laugh the loudest at a bar.
But you can't fuck the anxiety out
Of you,
even if you pretend to love fucking
lovers that you won't remember
or you wish you could forget.

We are sweaty and salty
looking for a path to follow
to the promised land they promised us.
So much of youth is spent
taking deep breaths to occupy our lungs,
thinking that there is always more air to
fill up our shallow selves,
yet still so terrified of running out of oxygen.
Death seems so far away,
shrouded in mystery
but our tragic selves are afraid of
Expiring our wasted youth.

Will we miss those early mornings
coming home at dawn
only to ourselves
seeking shelter from the cold
and wishing we had someone to hold.

The break

We are so careful with our hearts now
tiptoeing,
disillusioned.
where are the happily-ever-afters we were promised
we ate them up as children,
Perhaps we just couldn't process
The truth that the world is bitter.
I want you to know
That I gave it my all.
You used me all up
and I was glad for it.
I do not have to look back
and check if I walked the line.

I made a rope out of my hair to
pull you up towards me
my fingers were the steps
that carried your feet.

Dilemma
When you realize
that the one person
who can make you feel better
is the cause of your pain.

Empath PSA
I know why hermit crab goes back into its shell
it is not for the fear of the world
He can not fear something he carries on his back

it's so it can be kinder to itself
To heal its wounds
Because the atmosphere is harsh
and acidic
What a calamity it is to be a feeler

Some days it's like this

There is so much pain in the world. So much hurt.
Sometimes I question if little bits of darkness cover
kindness like dust particles
I constantly have to blow it away
remind myself, it's there. it's there.
I know nobody wants my tears. But they are there,
behind my eyes, just waiting.
I hear, don't cry, get angry about the injustice.
But that's just not in me.
It's an occasional, fleeting sugar rush
not mobilizing. not motivational.
a bright amber before it flows down my cheeks.
I was made weak,
pale and sickly emotional disposition.
I have to shield myself from the world, most days
because its words and images like to unravel me
And then I get swallowed by the void.

I don't believe in your revolution

Consider me defeated
I have no will to keep my fists up in this fight
There is no place for those in this resistance
that struggle just to keep their heads below the
clouds

Sensitive

It's so easy to lose me
One insult to the ego
and I want to disintegrate
My cells just mutually giving up on holding each
other
and in unison let go
I collapse into a bed like a wet lump of tissue

Attention Seeker

Why am I always hurting myself?
Do I simply use my body as a shield to ease the blows
of the world to my soul?
Physical pain is so much easier to process,
I choose being skinned to being left alone.

I would manage to find danger while covered in
bubble wrap
because you can't leave me as easily when you're
feeling bad for me,
because it's harder to walk away from someone
that's suffering,
And you can't turn your back on me
While my body is ill.

I am a horrible accident's single casualty
What a sad child I was to think this is happiness
To think I am only worthy of love when I am sick.

Red Flags

My feet are gripping
The shiny surface of the balance ball
On which I should give into freedom
Without losing my control

I should love hard and wholesome
But never smother and give it room to grow
I have to grow accustomed to this balance
In order for the ball to roll

I should stand up to life's bitter trials
And fight on to prove that I'm a worthy foe
But keep my composure and acceptance
Resign to knowing that I will eventually fall.

I keep stretching my own limits
I try to teach myself more about standing tall
But I am coming to a slow realization
Whether it is solid ground, a balance beam or a giant
rolling ball
I never learned to stand up on my own

Growing up is Giving up

I used to think that one day
Life is gonna go my way.
Surprise me
Magic really is real
It's everywhere around me
One day I'll stand up on a stage
And this is where I find you
The one who feels my pain
The one message
hit received
My bounty
Of everlasting happiness
Inside the path that I imagined

I don't dream that big anymore

Romanticism PSA

I am making headway killing brain cells
Cheering to the good old times
Thinking to myself that in my memories
I was always happier than now
But the past is always airbrushed
Time sands the blemishes away
I need to start liking
living in the worst parts of the present
And stop forgetting
That I was also miserable
then.

Pendulum Swings

I am so burnt out of ups and downs
One moment I am living my best life and hitting the
town
next minute I am contemplating self-harm
and plummet wearing a crown

Is it fair to taste so much grief in the air?
My dark sense of humor is just
melancholy undressing itself
What a cocktail it is, to feel so numb yet so at the
mercy of the motions.

Two Faced

My skull cracks in the middle
One part of my brain is the critic
The other is the victim
The left side contorts my face into a smile
The right side considers it fake and calls me a liar

Bystander PSA

I find myself found of
elaborate graffiti on the side of the moving train
voicemails from acquittances that want something
from you
Warm seats on trains
worn shoes with laces on the brink of extinction
unmade beds for their honesty and cheekiness
Fogged up bathroom mirrors
crumbs left on a plate like charted constellations
coffee stains on urgent paperwork read late into the
night
hair in my food
Fingerprints and lip-stains on wine glasses
Keyed car doors
Drunken piss in the elevator
Unfinished sandcastles or sandwiches
and
tire marks on a green lawn.

So far removed from participating in my own life
I am a spectator, finding traces of humanity,
like an alien studying an expired planet.
How destructive and captivating we are.
Oh, what a delight.

Pink Elephant

In the midst of depression:
You will always find yourself to be
an observer. Watching other people walk away from
your life. You will stand outside of bars, pretending to
wait on cars, drunk and wobbling from misery. You
will convince others that you got it together. Their
concern will taste like a mixture of pity and
embarrassment. You know that look. You saw it in
yourself just ten minutes ago in the mirror of a
graffitied bathroom.
...*want to make sure you get home safe*, they will tell
you. It will sound like they just don't want to feel
guilty if something were to happen.
I'm fine, really. You will shoot back at them. They
won't argue with you. They will be on their way to
the next bar or after-party. Leaving way too quick.
Leaving you to wish, they would have argued a little
longer, to be polite, at least.
You will throw your arm up in a sloppy wave in the
most ungraceful like manner. But they are not even
looking at you, struggling there, like a three-legged
animal.
Alone. The perceiver.

The fun stops too quick and the ground hits too hard
and you have never gotten this wasted of three
drinks before. The curb will feel cold under your ass
which is strange because you can't feel your cheeks
or the tips of your fingers.
1 thousand minutes later. Your ride is yet to arrive.
Sitting. By yourself. Recording the images.
Sometimes photographs, sometimes it's just images
that you burn inside of your brain to register the
exact details of this pathetic state that you are in.
And when the sadness sinks deep into your sweat
glands you will hold your own. Like your liquor.
Unappreciated. Wasted. Gram by gram ingested into
the wholesome of the universe. There is a good
chance you will fall asleep swallowing tears in the
back of the car.

One moment ago, you were just glad that you are alive. Glad, that you still manage to scrape the rusty wire framework that resembles a person off the floor into an upward position.
Next moment, you think to yourself that everything that you have ever done is wrong. Your own monologues repeat in your head and every word makes you nauseous. It could be the alcohol.
Why am I here?
Why isn't everyone sick of me?
I shall remain quiet. I will fade to the background.
Perhaps no one will notice how awful I am.
You make plans for the next day to avoid small talk and leave when no one notices. You are not sure what you are dreading more, the inevitability of the hangover or lunchtime when someone is to surely ask you if you are doing ok.
If you by some reckless, fiery miracle get home and manage to solicit the door to open you will fall asleep with a single thought:
I can't stand any minute of being myself.

Honesty

What is honesty, but falling to the knees of your own
self and weeping? You find it at the edges of your
own skin when there is nothing to save you from the
aching vibrations inside the cells of your flawed,
human nature. It waits for you like a whisper waits
until the room is silent and its presence becomes
heavy with purpose and at the right moment when
the buzzing of voices inside your head stops, you will
listen. Honesty does not shout, it has no need for
shouting. It tugs on your hairs, pinches your skin and
unravels you until you are no longer solid. It is not a
ticking clock or a ticking bomb. It won't haunt you
like thoughts of old age or loneliness. You are not
jailed by it, although sometimes you might feel like a
child running on a pier into the endless ocean. You
can not drown in it, honesty is in the air, it laces it
thinly, so many gasp until they are light-headed. For
many, it is hard to chew and sip it down as it scrapes
on the swollen parts of your ego, marked by years of
bearing grins and clutching onto the broken strings
of optimism. You are reminded, that you can't make
music out of broken instruments.

What is honesty, but looking at yourself in your own
true essence, as the mirror copies the tones of your
temperament and with eyes wide open, you are
holding your gaze.

When faced with disappointment

I like to remind myself
that I haven't been eaten alive by a cheetah
and there is a comfort in that

I like to put myself in spots
Where I can easily observe people
Who are so unaware of my pitfalls
And watch them as their days are spent and their
lives go by
So deliberately
So diligently
Despite my disappointment.

Cyclical Affliction

December is approaching.

I can feel it.
The night's cold breath inches closer to my ear.
I hear it eat away at daylight.

I feel as if I am awaiting an oncoming death of a poet.

I wrap myself in sweaters but
the shivers still run through my body.
My nostrils begin to exhale the winter.

People are a fickle distraction.
I surround myself with them
Only to find my seat taken.
I am vacant during this season

My independence
becomes a headless act of defiance
against my mutilated yearning.

My solitude
is a testament to lonesomeness
swelling in my blood cells
It is terminal cancer.

There is no running away.

All the sad songs
that are foreign to me
any other time of the year,
seem to pull on my wasting heart.

Epistle

Dear Deficient girl,
listening to love songs,
catching hopes like flies in the summer.
wishing and waiting
For someone to deliver you from your depressed
brain.

If you are waiting for a valourous rescue,
Stop.
It will not happen.
It's a rule-that is unbroken.

Every time you face the truth
you get cold shivers. like you are afraid
to admit to yourself that
your fears walk beside you
instead of your father
and there is no man waiting for you at the end.

Give it up. perhaps the world needs you hopeless
and scared, because it wants you for itself.
Jane Austen died alone and never married
neither did Queen Elizabeth.
and they were great.

Perhaps you will never stop wishing to be
a part of a complete, a set, like a pair of lungs.
You feel alone without your other.
A single headlight, shining in the dark.

But you won't admit it
and you will look up at ceilings
and suck in your tears on the edge of the eyelids.
Until your heart no longer beats

-Sincerely,
December

I don't know when my battery died

Fishing for compliments in
A steep pool of sarcasm,
she looks up with eyes so honest, color of Hennessy.
Seldom you will find such delicate coincidences
covered in healthy satin glow
sliding in-between slick silver linings.
December is an awful month for an epiphany.

Circling back

"Hello darkness my old friend"
plays inside my head.
This loss of appetite,
apathy,
restlessness,
my tired, veiny eyes...
are is so familiar.
The sleepless nights are almost a comfort blanket,
It has been almost 2 years
since I was hunted
by insomnia.
I was doing so well.
And I almost smile to myself,
I thought you unfriended me.

Creature Poem

There is a creature on my shoulder
That preys on every happy thought.
When I lay myself to rest at night,
He is the somber shiver down my spine.

His claws are on my collarbone.
His teeth have sunk above my breast.
He takes whatever joy he can from me.
In my own body, I become his guest.

When I am in the midst of laughter
He whispers to me, *you don't matter.*
When I receive a compliment
He whispers to me, *you are incompetent.*

And when I am putting on my makeup
He tilts the mirror and distorts the image
Until all I see is asymmetric imperfections.
He tells me, *smile darling, you are never good
enough.*

I try to never feed the creature
Although sometimes it just feels so good to wallow.
I fear to think that we are symbiotic
And without him suckling on my feelings, I won't
have compassion.

I never talk about the creature
I am ashamed that I have birthed a monster
I simply cradle him, with my arms around my knees
And dull his sharp teeth's numbing sorrow

Pleading Poem

There is a sadness inside me
that is hollow and bleak,
like a cup of black water.
It is pulling on me.

It smells like wet pavement,
on the rainiest days
but not like a thunderstorm
that carries the excitement.

When birds are chirping outside
and the weather is nice
I close all the curtains
and shut all the blinds.

I want to rest easy
And sleep off the blues
But I feel more and more tired
When I open my eyes

The princess at the bottom of the pond

I knew I was changing,
When I could fall asleep on trains
Better than in my own bed.
My uneasiness would dwindle
And my body would finally rest
Because at least it was moving forward.
Mother said the light behind my eyes was gone.
I am inclined to believe her,
Because my lead lungs are filled with water
and I'm laying somewhere where light
does not reach
Unless you struggle and swim upward
But I'm so tired...
I'm so tired...
That I don't even know which way is up.

Depressica

Life is swallowing weeks of my time
I can remember fragments
But not enough to go by
To identify
When I lost the grip on my mind
I keep telling myself the sun will come up
The sun will come up
And restore the life in my eyes

Morning Routine

Have you ever woken up in the morning, to put your
face on?
Not eyeliner to make your eyes bigger,
Or concealer to hide all your flaws.
It's putting on a smile instead of a frown.
It's opening your eyes wider so they don't see how
puffy they are
It's clearing your throat after you were weeping
during the night
it's practicing laughing since it's no longer a habit.

50mg

They looked into your eyes
to see if there was any Humanity left.
They said they need to continue the treatment.

Apologetic

I am trying to teach myself how to stop saying
"sorry"
by saying thank you,
by saying that's unfortunate,
by saying thanks for letting me know.

because I say it
as if I am apologizing for my existence.
But the truth is
I feel sorry it happened

The second law

Tiny
crystal
ballerina
dancing
on
the
edge.
Bright
red
peony
have
not
seen
rain
in
forty
weeks.
All
that
makes
me
whole
will
devour
me.
law
of
Entropy.

Suicide Fantasies

If I agree with myself to die
which is an argument we sporadically have,
I would like to die with my element.
Give myself to a brutish 10-foot wave
Have it tumble my body reckless into the churning
foam
Snap my neck with its military vigor
And drag me by the hair
across the sand and to the shore
Leave it beached and covered in salty froth.
That's how I would like to go.

No Title

I feel like dying.

Prey PSA

Like a tired bird
on a barbed wire
I have to choose
between the pain of holding on
and pain of tumbling to the ground

My wings are sore
from fluttering above the dirt
Not all feathered creatures are eagles
some are just anxious finches
That regret leaving the nest

Selfish Human

You don't tell a caged bird you are going to travel the
world
You just leave her

What does citizenship mean to you?

No longer being a caged bird,
finding a real home,
building it with a person I love.
Having the ability to go where my heart desires
and having the freedom to return.

Discipline PSA

Courage is a muscle
that must be practiced and
exercised with commitment and devotion.
Dedicate yourself to being brave,
for if your soul grows weak tissue of being
timid and afraid
the cruelty of the world
will make you into a helpless lamb.
Get ready
to be slaughtered
or worse, forgotten.

Wingless

I live in such a small world.
I am clawing at the walls.
Money is dripping like an IV,
Just enough to stay alert
but never to explore.
Sitting still in one place,
what a waste of youth.
Everyone is living to the fullest
but if I'm comparing
then I'm always losing
and you can't lose harder
than losing hope.

Hope

What is hope but a delusion that the odds will favor you? Do you hope about the sun rising? Why must you only trifle hope for uncertainty. Why not hope for cracks in concrete, turbulence on cloudy days, death, taxes, traffic and shitty managers. Those are the things you can depend on. These are the consistencies that will not delay but will deliver, probability be damned!
Why persist to feel so robbed and violated when things divert from plans when the agony is unavoidable and often so predictable. Agony is the natural erosion of the certainty that things will go your way. You make a deliberate tectonic shift in your perception of reality when you accept hope is the straw-like pillar that keeps the dread of reality from descending like poison from the atmosphere.

Hanged

Do you know that last scene in Shawshank
Redemption?
Where Morgan Freeman talks about hope and
"getting busy living"
or "getting busy dying"
and then he walks away from the room where
Brooks hanged himself
in that flea infested apartment that smelled like rot
and felt like your soul must have broken its own
knees
that it can't crawl out of misery and
you keep finding small places to suffocate yourself in
Red left only a carving of his name on a wall
No noose around his neck.

I have come to terms with it
I will probably never be a citizen
I will always be a subhuman form living in a country
of foreigners
but a stranger to my own people.
Fearful of tomorrow
but grateful for today.

I saw Red walk down the sandy beaches, with a big
old grin on his face
His tiny suitcase with his whole life neatly packed
and his shoes
slung over his shoulder
His hair grey but face so young
Wearing a tie for his first formal meeting with the
bluest of waters
I used to believe that he got out in the end
Now I believe that he is still a prisoner
Freedom is only a dying man's fever dream.

Caged in

I'm struggling.
Each day the cage is getting tighter.
I'm shedding all my feathers now
As metal bars are closing in around me.
Soon I'll have to make a choice
On how to use the remainder of the air.
I can take one
last
long
breath
hold my voice
And hope that I was a person worth remembering
Or I can use my last resolve
for the only thing that birds are capable of
And sing of sweet surrender.

Rape PSA

There were many times
I wished my rape was different
more theatrical
with me running down a trail in a park
streetlights illuminating my screams
as he violently chased me
salivating his hideousness
as it spills at the sides of his mouth.

My unsuspecting audience
of commuters passing by
become my rescuers
In moments just before I become a victim
I slip away like silk
with spectators tackling him to the ground
and beating a sense of justice
into his corrupted guts.

Denial made me replay my rape
each time with a different ending
hoping for anything
Instead of these plain apartment walls
this sullied mattress
and my body etching each painful detail
into the fabric of who I am.

My body
adjusting to the violation
by swallowing it whole and
neatly stacking the pain and the anger
into their very own compartments.

Arranging the broken parts of myself
to fit into smaller corners
so I can ask for less.

I thought my body was betraying me
but it just knew before I did that
I could never
unrape
myself.

And it had to keep on living.

Oh how I wish that instead of closed doors
to empty rooms where inebriated girls
become vacant trophies for self-assurance
and somber testaments to feeling wanted
you would know that devouring someone
won't make you feel any less
lonely.

Oh how I wish that rape could be reasoned with
as if I could caress your cruelty
to show you gentleness
to nurture your soul back from
its destructive ways.
Through tenderness
I teach you not to touch against my will.

And in a moment we are still
You change your mind
I seize my pleads and cries
and cradle the callous beast back into its keep.

I still find traces of your fingernails
imprinted on my the inside of my thighs
I have poured lakes upon my skin
but smell me,
do I still smell ruined to you?
I have forgiven myself for my rape
but have you?

Bye-Bye-Bicycle

I like to ride my bicycle,
I like to be by myself at times
No second passengers
Accompanied only by my thoughts

I like it when my rabid hair is foaming at the wind
I like when the gentle breeze touches my skin
he whispers to me
"That's a good girl..."

I flashback and convulse
and push the pedals faster
rolling the rubber tires through the pavement
the way his hand traced down my spinal cord

But just like the spinning wheels
leave a trail of dust following
some things no matter the distance traveled forward
cannot be escaped

It's funny, isn't it?
I gave my father figure two tries
and both have failed me.
I got two fathers for the price of not feeling like you
ever had one.
lucky girl
that always wished I could have been
a daddy's girl

I never cried about it,
into such delicate instruments, nature makes us little
females
they won't ever moan like violins
won't scream out painful melodies,
or screech like broken strings.
But they might apologize ever so constantly,
Or maybe they won't say anything

no reason to cry about things that seem normal
they don't know

that other daddies don't touch their daughters
like daddy touches you

Is this not rape?
It's something so deliberate
that made me wish that I never grew my breasts
so he wouldn't have to start again

It's funny isn't it?
Laugh with me, daddy issues are hilarious
but my childhood is no joke that
formed the woman that I am today

The fact that I can trust no man,
must be my fault
that I have concrete fears
but there are no solid walls to penetrate
when you are a broken girl

They say I most likely pick another daddy like you
who will also touch my little girl
But the only thing I can give birth to is flashbacks
How can I ever have room for a passenger?
when I can't even ride my bike solo
like a normal girl

Scraped Knees

I don't scrape my knees anymore
but when I did, it stung and I still had to take my
young ankles to the second floor.
I don't break my heart anymore
but when I did I still lived in a place where love was
possible
I don't get cold anymore
But when I did I welcomed sunshine on my skin
without abandon

I don't get to be brave anymore
Trauma took all my courage and replaced it with
caution.
I don't take risks anymore
Trauma makes a contingency plan for any
possibility of danger.
I don't mix my drinks anymore
Trauma watches them closely and sips liability
I don't sleep anymore
Trauma flashes images behind my eyelids instead of
dreams. They keep me restless.
I don't smile anymore
Trauma painted my face into a mime

Scraped Knees Part II

All that I am now is a grand theatrical performance
Locked into silence
Where I keep mouthing,
mutely screaming, "I'm gonna be okay"
This is a comedy of acting out the anxiety
Through body motions
And flinching at anybody's touch.
I am an artist of building unseen walls
And weeping without tears.
The others wonder why I am scraping at my face
I want to let them know
But the mask isn't coming off.

Aftermath PSA

Rape is the thief of the soul
beyond the violence of the act
It will drain you
And sap your spirit slowly

Rape is the thief of the voice
Everyone is scared of the word like a terminal illness
Like somehow saying R-A-P-E into the air
Is wishing it on someone

Rape is the thief of love
Giving up hope of being someone's else girl
anxious of having "that conversation"
reminding myself of the violation
and watching your interest wane

Violated

If I could be alive again
I would like to be a spider
Weave a web around my naked body
Hide me in a cocoon up higher
And let nobody harm me

Your last thoughts

I hope that day you ask yourself
have I lived
a life
worth living?
and then you remember
you are a fucking rapist.

Lacerations

Survival gave me wounds.
I gave myself stitches.
Watching myself in a mirror,
I had to sew my back closed
With a thread and a needle.
And even when my needlework was crooked
I never asked anyone's hand in assistance.

Only I am responsible for my scars healing.

Healing PSA

I am learning to lean into it:
to be more honest with each breath I take,
to show more kindness to myself
to forgive my false mistakes
and bend my ear close to silence
finding the echo of myself.

Despite the years of despising
how heartfelt was this overwhelming pain
It brings tears to my eyes to know
That in the times when I felt so alone
I had me all along.

Workplace PSA

Don't hold grudges.
Gather evidence.

Unprepared

In a valley of snakes
I am but a gentle lamb
Who can see the danger rustle through the grass
But won't move until there are teeth around my neck

Workplace politics

I made myself a comfortable nest
in a den full of snakes
Sleeping cozy with an adversary
Tucked me in with a knife in my back
You gave trust issues
To a trusting lamb
A big-eyed fool
With a heart like an envelope.
Your smiles
are done for profits
your chatter
is to get me to
Spread myself across the floor
So your feet have a warm place to sink into
You got me learning
When to stomp my heels
And hold my ground
Like I hold my head
And when to speak softly
Just to get your good graces
I like to like people
You like retaliation
I have to keep reminding myself
That you are not evil
You are just not good people

Anarchy in a Corporate Setting

I saw it with my own eyes:
The blank stare of being unable to place me,
The violent annoyance at my insubordination,
The grave disapproval of my disobedience.
Good girls don't question things.
Can't I fucking disagree with you and still be good?
Why do I have to give up parts of myself in order to
appease?
You want to crumble my spirit as if it is dry sand
Until the pieces fall back into the mold you made for
me

Women are just tools of trade in your hands
I don't care that you get promoted over me
Picking the fruits of my labor of my sweaty skin
Writing your name on the work I did
In the spaces, I left blank
You a rat in a maze chasing imaginary cheese they
will never give you
Do not for a second think that your salary makes you
better than me
We have to be equal for you to look me in the eyes
Small minds engage in cockfights to hide their
inferior dick size

Death PSA

How am I supposed to do this?
How am I supposed to breathe
when my lungs are full of glass
Although I am shattered
each piece of me still shines
each ray of sunlight is reflecting
of the fragments of who I was
How am I supposed to get better
when I have no words to fill the void
not a single tear will turn solid
each one demands a cheek to burn
How do I keep going?
In a world without your love.

Aloe vera

I have this plant
that was dying until you watered it
I see it green now
On my windowsill
And I catch myself having a thought
That I must that keep that plant alive
At all costs
I'm clutching
To this plant
To take control over death
And I realize that nothing is permanent
I can't save the plant if it's not willing to live
Like I couldn't save you.

Missing You

The essence of you
is packed in the scent of
this old, ugly sweater.
I never dare to wear
because I'm afraid that
it will smell of me
instead of you.
I don't want to lose this last trace.
Holding on to objects
Is a way to hold on to people
When the weight of missing them
Doesn't seem to have limits.
I bet in your eyes
I'm still a turtledove
splashing water in deepest of puddles
and you would never expect me to grow
into a girl who is burying bobby pins in the carpet
and afraid of making mistakes.

Olga

I would give up my sight for 5 days
And fast for seven
And not speak ill of anyone for ten years
And forgive every offense as if I swallow thick
needles
I would walk for a day without taking a moment's
break,
kneel before any Gods or demons or Kings or beggars
And drink up dirt at their command
I would scratch, heal and scar and scratch again a
maze into my back
Follow those lines like a map
To a moment where we lay next to each other and
you tell me all the secrets that you took with you
Death is a heavy shroud
But it won't tip the scale of my lingering guilt
But somewhere the Gods or the demons or the Kings
or the beggars
Swallow lifetimes
And I just want you to whisper farewell.

Grieving PSA

You left me with so much pain
So much pain I can't even turn it into anything
Not art
Not poetry
At least not any good

The Great War

For 19 days and 20 nights
We stood on our knees until they were bloodied
Bowing our heads low to their boots with tears in our
eyes
We prayed and we begged for them to give us the
bodies
Their eyes are still open
their souls can't find a way back.

As if the starvation wasn't enough suffering
As if one day I can unsee this war
They cut off my love's fist
And then made his hand knock on my door
First time in four years I heard my heart jumping
As I pressed his cold hand against my warm throat
I once was a child when I heard
"The Germans are coming"
I am afraid
I am a human no more

Mantra: For a friend

Be brave small soul
For your breaths are short
And your steps are
So uncertain.
The rough framing of the world
Will growl and gnaw at you
So very often.
You will find that it takes more
Than sheer strength
To lead a path of kindness
And when you are starting to lose hope
You will find it
Right beside you.

Change PSA

Change is a hollow difficult process
That must be practiced with commitment
and precision of a Japanese tea ceremony.
The muscle of change must be exercised and pushed
to new baselines. You will find resistance to change
in others but most devastatingly and often at a
surprise, yourself. Your mind, your body, your spirit
is a stubborn foe that you will have to wrestle
into submission.

Mantra: For Myself

I am free and I live with no reservations.
I allow myself to be reckless and unapologetic.
I rush in fully and foolishly and often so quickly that
my own intentions are not clear to me.
I made mistakes and I forgive myself.
I don't wish to live a timid existence, to be unnoticed
in quiet solitude as days pass me by. I want to carve
my own path, heroically as I run with my heart open.
Yes, I may be vulnerable and tragic but I embrace the
pain of honesty and attachment.
I long to love those around me unhinged, unburdened
and unsolicited.
Stripped of mistrust and lack of faith I stand by, loyal
to chase the eternal summer.

Advice to a friend #1

It's good to rub against the edges of your heart,
To know how deep it is, what it is capable of.
How it twists and cringes and winces.
How it shifts and hooks under pressure.
Sometimes you need to let the sadness carve a deep
opening in you,
that makes you into a hollow basin.
You will find that you are bottomless.
In moments when you are about to spurt and drip
down your margins,
You will bear so much more
And marvel at how vast you are.
All that space you created can be filled with delight.
It will fill all the crevices, corners and aspects that
you never could have reached,
had you remained numb to the pain.

Advice to a friend #3

Do not shame the girl
Who cringes every time she looks in the mirror.
Someone painted her into a monster
And every day she has to relive it.
It's easier for her to make love
with the lights off
and kiss with eyes closed
So you can see the real her.

Advice to a friend #4

Don't give up.
It's a bad situation, not a bad life.
You will swim to the shore.
I'll get in the water with you if I need to. No matter
how cold.

Advice to friend #5

Do not be scared of pain or love. Either of them will
find you. You can not hide or control that. They have
been eating people up for much longer than you have
been around.

Advice to Self
Read
And
Dwell
And
Produce
And
Fail
And
Feel.

In defense of cardiology

If you lay there long enough
You might notice the slight vibrations
your body makes as your heart pulsates through your
body.
11 ounces of shivery flesh
fighting an uphill battle
against the time and hazards of human existence.

Cut it some slack,
when faced with whaling tremors in your soul
when you are ill with life's tendency to deliver
disappointments
and you are repulsed with the meaty suit you wear
like a costume
it still beats.

On figuring it out

- ❏ Trust the process
- ❏ ~~Trust the Struggle~~

A plea to humanity

When your ribs are cracked under the heaviness of
circumstance
Do good

When misfortune makes a nest in your bed and
steals your covers
Do good

When the ones you trusted have chosen to take the
unexpected yet satisfyingly selfish act of skimming
the truth
Do good

Do good against all odds, despite your better
judgment
in times when your calloused fingers are about to
lose grip

Because we are born into a world that is always
falling short of everything that we deserve as human
beings
and despite that this planet has natural treasure and
abundance, greed has leeched it almost dry
and as a child you one day lost your innocence to
learning the abhorrent history of the holocaust, rape,
slavery, torture, witch-trials, and pointless wars.

So when you are worn down and demoralized by the
small and major bullshit of the world and ready to
strike back with vengeance and retaliate at the
unfairness and injustice that was shown to you
ask
is there any room for more pain in this world?

Do good
it is the only way to do right by yourself.

Let it Go

There is beauty in the fleeting:
in the things that do not last,
in the ripeness of the fruit that turns sweet than sour,
in the gust of wind, that blurred away
the pollen of the dandelion

On How to Keep Going

The trick to life is knowing the hard parts
They are unavoidable
Like corners of the table
If you trace your fingers long enough around the
edge
Eventually, you will hit one

You have all the power
if you know that this isn't hell
or the end of days
it's only the hard part.

Too often I found myself slip
and slide into depression
since I resume to think that
it can not get better than this
and I am stuck living the same
miserable groundhog day
of waking up and
going to sleep wanting to kill myself.

Knowing your enemy is half the battle.

Thank you,
Al

Made in the USA
Columbia, SC
30 December 2019